… and Just Begun!

The Party Is Over
... and Just Begun!

Almost Anonymous

A. Nonnie Muss

Editor J.R. Fisher

Rhymestone Arts
Sequim, WA

Dedicated to the members
of my following Home Groups:

The Sequim Early Birds
The Joyce Way Out Group
and the Sequim Attitude Adjustment
Breakfast Meeting

and
to AA members everywhere
in the world

Copyright 2014
Rhymestone Arts
Sequim, WA

Table of Contents

Table of Contents v
Introduction 1
Preface and Forewords 3
The Doctor's Opinion 8
Bill's Story 12
There Is a Solution 30
More About Alcoholism 33
We Agnostics 37
How It Works 42
Into Action 60
Working with Others 66
To Wives 67
The Family Afterwards 69
To Employers 72
A Vision for You 73
Personal Stories 75
Appendix I 90
Appendix II 92
Afterword 96

Introduction

This book is the result of over thirty years of Post It notes and scribbles on napkins. Whenever something struck me as funny in an AA pitch, I jotted it down. Arranging these gems into some sort of sensible order was the hard part. But what better way than to follow the structure of the Big Book itself?

At the top of each page, you'll find a quote from the Big Book that should support and/or inspire the poems on that same page. Some of the poems might be a little bit of a stretch. Remember that we love to laugh in AA, but we might not all laugh at the same things or for the same reasons. Take what you like and leave the rest.

The longest section is "Bill's Story." To me, this makes perfect sense because it was his story that began my own identification as an alcoholic. It might have been the same for you. At the end of the book, I've included some of my favorite stories, no matter which of the four editions they were taken from. At the beginning of the book, I've included material from the preface and forewords to all of the editions because of the rich history they contain.

The title is deliberately chosen. The boozing, alcoholic party is definitely over, but the real party, meaning the sober life, filled with laughter and joy, is just beginning! We are a happy, joyous and free people. If this book contributes just one laugh along the way, then it has done its job.

THE PARTY IS OVER ...

I am glad that I've lived long enough and stayed sober long enough to see AA spread throughout the world. The language might be different from meeting to meeting, but the laughter is the same!

Enjoy! Jim F

... AND JUST BEGUN!

We, of Alcoholics Anonymous, are more than one hundred men and women who have recovered from a seemingly hopeless state of mind and body. To show other alcoholics precisely how we have recovered is the main purpose of this book. For them, we hope these pages will prove so convincing that no further authentication will be necessary.
 — *Foreword to the First Edition (1939)*

We are not

an organization in the conventional sense
   of the word.

There are no fees or
   dues whatsoever.

The only requirement for membership is an honest desire to stop
   drinking.

We are not allied with any particular faith, sect or denomination, nor do we oppose
   anyone.

We simply wish to be helpful to those who are
   afflicted.

Anonymous

It is important that we remain anonymous because we are too few, at present to handle

the overwhelming number of personal appeals which may result from this publication.

THE PARTY IS OVER ...

The spark that was to flare into the first A.A. group was struck at Akron, Ohio, in June 1935, during a talk between a New York stockbroker and an Akron physician.
— *Foreword to Second Edition (1955)*

Our Hope

It is our
great hope that
all those who
have as yet
found no answer
may begin
to find one
in the pages
of this book
and will presently
join us on
the high road
to a new
freedom.

Since the original

foreword
to
this
book
was
written
in
1939,

a
wholesale
miracle
has
taken
place.

... AND JUST BEGUN!

The basic principles of the A.A. program, it appears, hold good for individuals with many different lifestyles, just as the program has brought recovery to those of many different nationalities. The Twelve Steps that summarize the program may be called los Doce Pasos in one country, les Douze Etapes in another, but they trace exactly the same path to recovery that was blazed by the earliest members of Alcoholics Anonymous.
— Foreword to the Third Edition (1976)

Personal

In spite
of
the great
increase

in the size
and
the span
of this
Fellowship,

at its core
it remains
simple
and
personal.

Keep It Simple

Each day,
somewhere
in the world,
recovery

begins
when one
alcoholic
talks

with another
alcoholic,
sharing
experience,

strength,
and hope.

THE PARTY IS OVER ...

All changes made over the years in the Big Book (A.A. members' fond nickname for this volume) have had the same purpose: to represent the current membership of Alcoholics Anonymous more accurately, and thereby to reach more alcoholics. If you have a drinking problem, we hope that you may pause in reading one of the forty-four personal stories and think ...
 — *Preface to the Third Edition (1976)*

Yes

I've
felt
like
that.

Yes,
I
believe
this
program
can
work
for
me,
too.

Still One Sixty-Four

Because this book
has become the basic text
for our Society
and has helped such large
numbers of alcoholic
men and women to recovery,
there exists a sentiment
against any radical changes
being made in it.

Therefore, the first
portion of this volume,
describing the A.A. recovery
program, has been left
untouched.

... AND JUST BEGUN!

This fourth edition of "Alcoholics Anonymous" came off press in November 2001, at the start of a new millennium. Since the third edition was published in 1976, worldwide membership of A.A. has just about doubled, to an estimated two million or more, with nearly 100,800 groups meeting in approximately 150 countries around the world.
    — Foreword to Fourth Edition (2001)

Literature

has played
a major role
in A.A.'s growth,
and a striking

phenomenon
of the past
quarter-century
has been

the explosion
of translations
of our basic
literature

into many
languages and
    dialects.

Meetings

In any meeting,
anywhere, A.A.'s
share experience,
strength, and hope
with each other, in
order to stay
sober and help other
alcoholics.

Modem-to-modem
or face-to-face,
A.A.'s speak
the language
of the heart in all
its power and
    simplicity.

THE PARTY IS OVER ...

The physician who, at our request, gave us this letter, has been kind enough to enlarge upon his views in another statement which follows. In this statement he confirms what we who have suffered alcoholic torture must believe—that the body of the alcoholic is quite as abnormal as his mind.
  — The Doctor's Opinion, page xxiv

Denial

I
don't
have
Attention
Deficit
Disorder,
it's
just—

Oh,
look!
It's
a
bunny
rabbit!

Normal Is

I don't drink,
normally.

You see,
I did not
get into trouble
every time
I drank,

but every
time I
got into trouble,
I had been
drinking.

I don't drink
normally.

... AND JUST BEGUN!

Men and women drink essentially because they like the effect produced by alcohol. The sensation is so elusive that, while they admit it is injurious, they cannot after a time differentiate the true from the false. To them, their alcoholic life seems the only normal one.
— The Doctor's Opinion, page xxvi

Opportunity

may
knock
just
once,

but
temptation
will
bang

on
your
front
door

for
ever.

Likes

I
really
don't
like
alcohol
anymore,

but
I
don't
like
it
any
less,
either.

THE PARTY IS OVER ...

They are restless, irritable and discontented, unless they can again experience the sense of ease and comfort which comes at once by taking a few drinks — drinks which they see others taking with impunity.
   — The Doctor's Opinion, page xxvi-vii

Reaching the Bottom

Restless,
irritable,
and
  discontent,

stupid,
boring,
and
  glum,

pitiful
and
incomprehensible
  demoralization,

are
we
having
  fun?

Snickers

In
AA,
they
say—

some
times
you
feel
like
a
nut,

some
times
you
  don't.

... AND JUST BEGUN!

I earnestly advise every alcoholic to read this book through, and though perhaps he came to scoff, he may remain to pray.
— *The Doctor's Opinion, page xxx*

Education

Smart
men
learn
from
their
own
mistakes,

wise
men
from
the
mistakes
of
others.

The Future

I
don't
know
what
the
future
holds,

but
I
know
who
holds
the
future.

THE PARTY IS OVER ...

War fever ran high in the New England town to which we new, young officers from Plattsburg were assigned, and we were flattered when the first citizens took us to their homes, making us feel heroic. Here was love, applause, war; moments sublime with intervals hilarious. I was part of life at last, and in the midst of the excitement I discovered liquor.
— *Chapter 1: Bill's Story, page 1*

Kamikaze

Did
you
hear
about

the
famous
kamikaze
pilot

who
once
flew
thirty-seven

successful
missions?

On February First

Dressed in purple robes
of self-importance,
I feel the quick red kick
of booze settle into

the mellow yellow glow
of some great blue escape,
hot pink companionship
of other drinkers,

but I always forget
the black cloud of remorse,
the bright white pain
of the hangover,

to say nothing
about the horror of facing
another grey day.

... AND JUST BEGUN!

Though my drinking was not yet continuous, it disturbed my wife. We had long talks when I would still her forebodings by telling her that men of genius conceived their best projects when drunk; that the most majestic constructions of philosophic thought were so derived.
— Chapter 1: Bill's Story, page 2

Faith

Every
one
needs
some
thing
to
believe
in.

I
believe
I'll
have
another
beer.

An Ode

O, silver gin
of easy feelings,
gold vermouth
    of false comfort,

hour glass
of sophistication,
once guzzled
    with impunity,

now stirred
by this swizzle stick
    of restlessness,

olive skewered
upon the toothpick
    of irritability,

hope lying soggy
on the napkin
    of discontent.

THE PARTY IS OVER ...

The papers reported men jumping to death from the towers of High Finance. That disgusted me. I would not jump. I went back to the bar. My friends had dropped several million since ten o'clock—so what? Tomorrow was another day. As I drank, the old fierce determination to win came back.
— Chapter 1: Bill's Story, page 4

Life

isn't
about
how
to
survive
the
storm,

but
how
to
dance
in
the
rain.

Passion

When
the
passion
fades

you'll
need
a
lot
of
money

to
take
its
place.

... AND JUST BEGUN!

No words can tell of the loneliness and despair I found in that bitter morass of self-pity. Quicksand stretched around me in all directions. I had met my match. I had been overwhelmed. Alcohol was my master.
— *Chapter 1: Bill's Story, page 8*

Proverb

I
have
learned
that
whatever
hits
the
fan

it
will
never
be
evenly
distributed.

Sick and Tired

I've
learned
that
you
can
keep
on
puking

long
after
you
think
you're
finished.

THE PARTY IS OVER ...

How dark it is before the dawn! In reality that was the beginning of my last debauch. I was soon to be catapulted into what I like to call the fourth dimension of existence. I was to know happiness, peace, and usefulness, in a way of life that is incredibly more wonderful as time passes.
— *Chapter 1: Bill's Story, page 8*

Holidays

If
you
want
a
safe
Fourth
of
July,

don't
buy
a
fifth

on
the
    third.

Faith

is
like
a
bungee
cord,

let
go,

but
trust
in
the
laws
of
physics.

... AND JUST BEGUN!

He looked straight at me. Simply, but smilingly, he said, "I've got religion." I was aghast. So that was it—last summer an alcoholic crackpot; now, I suspected, a little cracked about religion. He had that starry-eyed look. Yes, the old boy was on fire all right. But bless his heart, let him rant! Besides, my gin would last longer than his preaching.
— *Chapter 1: Bill's Story, page 9*

I am

I are
the way
I am

you be
the way
you is

they be
the way
they do

we walk
the talk

do be
do be
do

Arrested Alcoholics

Idling in
a retrogressive
groove

is like
an old Eddie Arnold
album with a scratch:

Oh, lonesome me ...
[click]

Oh, lonesome me ...
[click]

Oh, lonesome me ...
[click]

Oh, lonesome me ...
[click]

All night long ...

THE PARTY IS OVER ...

He had come to pass his experience along to me—if I cared to have it. I was shocked, but interested. Certainly I was interested. I had to be, for I was hopeless.
 — *Chapter 1: Bill's Story, pages 9-10*

Kindergarten in AA

Stop drinking,
sit on your hands,
play solitaire,
and don't fall in love.

Look before
you leap, not after,
see the forest
and not just the trees.

Listen up,
take the cotton out
of your ears,
put it in your mouth.

Hold hands when you
cross the street,
    and do not jaywalk.

Bar Life

Indeed, I am
the center
of the universe.

How could
it be any other
way?

Like rings
on a dart board,
I send ripples

around the room,
and the world
sends back

darts as my sole
reward.

... AND JUST BEGUN!

I had always believed in a Power greater than myself. I had often pondered these things. I was not an atheist. Few people really are, for that means blind faith in the strange proposition that this universe originated in a cipher and aimlessly rushes nowhere.
— *Chapter 1: Bill's Story, page 10*

The Group

In
AA
the
whole
group
really
is
greater

than
the
sum
of
its
parts.

In and Out

Breathe
in,
breathe
  out.

Peace
in,
war
  out.

Love
in,
hate
  out.

God
in,
committee
  out.

THE PARTY IS OVER ...

How could there be so much of precise and immutable law, and no intelligence? I simply had to believe in a Spirit of the Universe, who knew neither time nor limitation. But that was as far as I had gone.
— Chapter 1: Bill's Story, page 10

Buddhism

—Amy Tan

The
river
of
happiness
always
flows

into
the
salty
tears

of
the
great
sea.

Swim

It
is
far
easier

to
swim
down
stream

than
have
to
fight

the
current.

... AND JUST BEGUN!

My ideas about miracles were drastically revised right then. Never mind the musty past; here sat a miracle directly across the kitchen table. He shouted great tidings.
— Chapter 1: Bill's Story, page 11

Optimism

If
your
life
is
a
pile
of
shit,

there
must
be
a
pony
some
    place.

Suit up

I
wear
sobriety
like
a
loose
garment.

I
wore
drunkenness
like
a
strait
jacket.

THE PARTY IS OVER ...

I could go for such conceptions as Creative Intelligence, Universal Mind or Spirit of Nature but I resisted the thought of a Czar of the Heavens, however loving His sway might be. I have since talked with scores of men who felt the same way.

My friend suggested what then seemed a novel idea. He said, "Why don't you choose your own conception of God?"

— Chapter 1: Bill's Story, page 12

In the Book

In the name
of Yahweh, find
the word we,

and in Jesus
you'll see the us,
while Allah
holds all,

so that we,
meaning all of us,
are People
of the Book,

and just brothers
fighting
over marbles.

Chapel by the Lake

The walls are pine,
the floor a carpet of green,
the ceiling vaulted
as high as the very sky,

the pews, rough-hewn logs
and stumps of trees,
the bells are wind-chimes
in the morning breeze,

the incense is the smoke
of the campfire,
the choir is dressed in robes
of grey and teal,

as the congregation
flies in for the communion
      meal.

... AND JUST BEGUN!

Never was I to pray for myself, except as my requests bore on my usefulness to others. Then only might I expect to receive. But that would be in great measure.
— *Chapter 1: Bill's Story, page 13*

Philosophy

Bloom where
you're planted,
play the hand
you're dealt,

drink your juice,
eat your toast,
do first
things first,

and when life
comes up lemons,
make lemonade,

go to the mound,
wind up, let go
    and let God.

Laws of Alcoholic Metaphysics

First of all,
you have
to give it away
    to keep it,

lose
everything
in order
    to win,

be powerless
before
you can
    be strong,

and drink
into a blackout
if you want
    to see the light.

THE PARTY IS OVER ...

Simple, but not easy; a price had to be paid. It meant destruction of self-centeredness. I must turn in all things to the Father of Light who presides over us all.
— Chapter 1: Bill's Story, page 13

AA Adages

One day at a time
you just follow the line,
keep it simple, dummy,
feed your tummy,

because easy does it
means now, not was it,
and think, think, think
is not drink, drink,
   drink,

so let go, let God,
and don't spoil the rod,
turn it over, Grover,
it's nothing but clover,

and keep coming back,
in spite of the flack.

Alcoholic Basketball

As I was driving
to the basket
for an easy lay-in,

I jumped up
and blocked my
own shot,

and later,
when I thought
I had been fouled,

instead of going
to the line
for a free-throw,

I sat on the bench,
and cried.

... AND JUST BEGUN!

I felt lifted up, as though the great clean wind of a mountain top blew through and through. God comes to most men gradually, but His impact on me was sudden and profound.
— *Chapter 1: Bill's Story, page 14*

The Way

For
the
spiritual
climber,

there
are
many
paths

to
the
top

of
the
mountain.

Showers

The
grace
of
God
comes
like
the
rain,

whether
you
want
it
or
not.

THE PARTY IS OVER ...

Faith without works was dead, he said. And how appallingly true for the alcoholic! For if an alcoholic failed to perfect and enlarge his spiritual life through work and self-sacrifice for others, he could not survive the certain trials and low spots ahead. If he did not work, he would surely drink again, and if he drank, he would surely die. Then faith would be dead indeed. With us it is just like that.
— *Chapter 1: Bill's Story, pages 14-15*

Faith

Fear
may
just
be
a
lack
of
denial

and
not
the
loss
of
faith.

Change

If
you
don't
change,

your
sobriety
date
will.

It
works,

if
you
work
it ...

... AND JUST BEGUN!

In one western city and its environs there are one thousand of us and our families. We meet frequently so that newcomers may find the fellowship they seek. At these informal gatherings one may often see from 50 to 200 persons. We are growing in numbers and power.
— Chapter 1: Bill's Story, pages 15-16

Kiss

Keep
it
simple
stupid,

just
go
to
meetings,

and
do
not
drink

in
between.

Meetings

Twenty
losers
meet
for
an
hour
every
day,

then
twenty
winners
go
their
way.

THE PARTY IS OVER ...

An alcoholic in his cups is an unlovely creature. Our struggles with them are variously strenuous, comic, and tragic. One poor chap committed suicide in my home. He could not, or would not, see our way of life.
— *Chapter 1: Bill's Story, page 16*

Unlovely

An
alcoholic
in
his
cups
is
an
unlovely
creature.

But
he
would
not
agree.

Choices

Happy
joyous
and
free,

stupid
boring
and
glum,

not
an
easy
choice

for
some.

... AND JUST BEGUN!

Most of us feel we need look no further for Utopia. We have it with us right here and now. Each day my friend's simple talk in our kitchen multiplies itself in a widening circle of peace on earth and good will to men.

— *Chapter 1: Bill's Story, page 16*

Slips

When
Daniel
escaped
from
the
lion's
den,

he
didn't
go
back
for
his
coat.

Service

Ask
not
what
AA
can
do
for
you,

but
what
you
can
do
for
AA.

THE PARTY IS OVER ...

The tremendous fact for every one of us is that we have discovered a common solution. We have a way out on which we can absolutely agree, and upon which we can join in brotherly and harmonious action. This is the great news this book carries to those who suffer from alcoholism.
 — *Chapter 2: There Is a Solution, page 17*

The First Time

The alley was pitch black,
and I, hungover something fierce.
Why me? I thought, as our feet
scrunched on the gravel,
the smell from the dumpster
nauseating.

It's just up ahead, she said,
the one I'd called the night before.

We climbed the rickety,
unpainted steps to the back door,
then suddenly we were inside
with the laughter, the bright lights,
and the warm hands—
I was home.

... AND JUST BEGUN!

The fact is that most alcoholics, for reasons yet obscure, have lost the power of choice in drink. Our so-called will power becomes practically nonexistent. We are unable, at certain times, to bring into our consciousness with sufficient force the memory of the suffering and humiliation of even a week or a month ago. We are without defense against the first drink.
— *Chapter 2: There Is a Solution, page 24*

The tremendous fact

for every one of us
is that we have
discovered
a common solution.

We have a way out
on which we can
absolutely agree,
and upon which
we can join in brotherly
and harmonious action.

This is the great news
this book carries
to those who suffer
from alcoholism.

Alcoholics

Is it true
your neighbor
died
last week?

Yes, it was
all the drinking
finally
did him in.

I'm so sorry.
Isn't it a shame
he never
found AA?

Oh, he wasn't
that bad.

THE PARTY IS OVER ...

The central fact of our lives today is the absolute certainty that our Creator has entered into our hearts and lives in a way which is indeed miraculous. He has commenced to accomplish those things for us which we could never do by ourselves.
 — *Chapter 2: There Is a Solution, page 25*

Hail Mary

full
of
grace,
I'm
late
to
the
meeting,

and
could
use
a
parking
place!

The Golden Years

Our life is
not measured

by the number
of breaths

we take,
but by the moments

that take
our breath away.

Never regret
becoming older

because
too many of us

are denied
the privilege!

... AND JUST BEGUN!

Most of us have been unwilling to admit we were real alcoholics. No person likes to think he is bodily and mentally different from his fellows. Therefore, it is not surprising that our drinking careers have been characterized by countless vain attempts to prove we could drink like other people.
— *Chapter 3: More about Alcoholism, page 30*

Wisdom

For
God's

sake,
if

you're
going

through
hell,

don't
stop

to
pitch

a
tent.

Three Ways

There are
three ways
to get
something
done —

do it
yourself,
hire
someone,

or tell
an alcoholic
not
to do
it.

THE PARTY IS OVER ...

Here are some of the methods we have tried: Drinking beer only, limiting the number of drinks, never drinking alone, never drinking in the morning, drinking only at home, never having it in the house, never drinking during business hours, drinking only at parties, switching from scotch to brandy, drinking only natural wines, agreeing to resign if ever drunk on the job, taking a trip, not taking a trip ...
— Chapter 3: More about Alcoholism, page 31

A Walking Contradiction

Acting as if
I knew, or acting as if
I didn't care,
as if life were all black
or all white,

either an either or
or an all yes or an all no
experience,
simply put: either I had it,
or I didn't have it,

but when I got it,
I no longer wanted it—
full of booze,
I was running on empty.

Monkey

The monkey on my back is still here,

just under my chair, doing pushups.

... AND JUST BEGUN!

But the actual or potential alcoholic, with hardly an exception, will be absolutely unable to stop drinking on the basis of self-knowledge.
  — Chapter 3: More about Alcoholism, page 39

Speared

I started out as a cucumber,
green, but solid and tight-skinned,
very good for family salads.

Then, in my teen years, I got
a little pickled on beer and wine,
but I was still plenty sweet.

Later, I relished the neighborhood
barbecues, hot dogs on a stick,
and falling down drunk.

But my moods got more sour
as I moved into vats of hard liquor,
not really kosher, but fun.

Or so I told myself, knowing
it was far too late to go back and be
 a cucumber again.

THE PARTY IS OVER ...

Once more: The alcoholic at certain times has no effective mental defense against the first drink. Except in a few rare cases, neither he nor any other human being can provide such a defense. His defense must come from a Higher Power.
— Chapter 3: More about Alcoholism, page 43

Wet Behind the Ears

The
spiritual
part
of
the
program
is
like

the
wet
part
of
the
ocean.

Wants

In AA
I've always
been given
exactly
what
I needed,

only then
to discover
later on

that it
was what
I really
wanted
all along.

... AND JUST BEGUN!

In the preceding chapters you have learned something of alcoholism. We hope we have made clear the distinction between the alcoholic and the non-alcoholic. If, when you honestly want to, you find you cannot quit entirely, or if when drinking, you have little control over the amount you take, you are probably alcoholic. If that be the case, you may be suffering from an illness which only a spiritual experience will conquer.
— *Chapter 4: We Agnostics, page 44*

Zero   Hero

—the drinking game

one	fun
two	blue
three	spree
four	more
five	jive
six	tricks
eight	wait
seven	heaven
ten	then
twelve	elves
nine	divine
fourteen	mean
seven	eleven
thirteen	green

THE PARTY IS OVER ...

To one who feels he is an atheist or agnostic such an experience seems impossible, but to continue as he is means disaster, especially if he is an alcoholic of the hopeless variety. To be doomed to an alcoholic death or to live on a spiritual basis are not always easy alternatives to face.
— *Chapter 4: We Agnostics, page 44*

We Agnostics

Jews
do not recognize
Jesus
as the savior.

Protestants
do not recognize
the pope
as the leader
of the Christian
church.

Baptists
do not recognize
each other
at the liquor store.

... AND JUST BEGUN!

Lack of power, that was our dilemma. We had to find a power by which we could live, and it had to be a Power greater than ourselves. Obviously. But where and how were we to find this Power?
— Chapter 4: We Agnostics, page 45

Today

I
will
start
living
from
the
inside
out,

instead
of
from
the
outside
in.

Eternal

If
you
want
to
get
to
the
eternal,

you
first
have
to
go
internal.

THE PARTY IS OVER ...

When we became alcoholics, crushed by a self-imposed crisis we could not postpone or evade, we had to fearlessly face the proposition that either God is everything or else He is nothing. God either is, or He isn't. What was our choice to be?
— *Chapter 4: We Agnostics, page 53*

Serenity Prayer

God
grant me
the serenity

to accept
the things
I cannot
change,

courage
to change
the things
I can,

and wisdom
to know
the difference.

Prayer

Thank
you,
Lord,
for
all
you've
given
me

and
for
all
you've
taken
away!

... AND JUST BEGUN!

We finally saw that faith in some kind of God was a part of our make-up, just as much as the feeling we have for a friend. Sometimes we had to search fearlessly, but He was there. He was as much a fact as we were. We found the Great Reality deep down within us. In the last analysis it is only there that He may be found. It was so with us.
— Chapter 4: We Agnostics, page 55

Circularities

When I was young
I had fun by spinning
around in circles
    until I dropped.

When I was older
I made bold with booze
and drank and drank
    until I dropped.

When I was wise
as a disguise, I argued
in circles all day
    until I dropped.

When I was done
I sucked on this thumb
and cried and cried
    until I stopped.

Hedge Your Bets

Stick
with
the
winners

at
the
meeting
place

learn
to
show

your
smiling
face.

THE PARTY IS OVER ...

Rarely have we seen a person fail who has thoroughly followed our path. Those who do not recover are people who cannot or will not completely give themselves to this simple program, usually men and women who are constitutionally incapable of being honest with themselves.
  — Chapter 5: How It Works, page 58

Disease of Alcoholism

When they said,
This is a disease
of denial,

I said,
No, it's not!

When they said,
This is a disease
of isolation,

I said,
Leave me alone!

When they said,
This is a disease
of loneliness,

I nodded and
  stayed to listen.

Little Things

Confucius
say
it
is
not
the
elephants
that
get
you,

but
those
pesky
ants.

... AND JUST BEGUN!

The Twelve Steps of Alcoholics Anonymous

Here are the steps we took, which are suggested as a program of recovery:

1. We admitted we were powerless over alcohol — that our lives had become unmanageable.

Powerless

Alcohol

The	is
man	the
takes	universal
a	solvent,
drink;	
	it
The	can
drink	remove
takes	anything,
a	
drink;	inhibitions,
	clothes,
The	wives,
drink	children,
takes	
the	money,
man.	careers.

THE PARTY IS OVER ...

The Twelve Steps of Alcoholics Anonymous

Here are the steps we took, which are suggested as a program of recovery:

2. Came to believe that a Power greater than our- selves could restore us to sanity.

I Believe

Our mind

I could not hear
what I could not hear,

I could not see
what I could not see,

I could not know
what I could not know,

I could not feel
what I could not feel,

until my ears
and eyes were open,

until my mind
and heart were open,

only then could I come
to believe.

is
like
an
onion,

each
day
we
peel

away
one
more
layer

of
delusion.

... AND JUST BEGUN!

The Twelve Steps of Alcoholics Anonymous

Here are the steps we took, which are suggested as a program of recovery:

3. Made a decision to turn our will and our lives over to the care of God as we understood Him

Power	AA Prayer
The	Thy
task	will
ahead	be
of	done
us	
	because
is	if
never	my
as	will
great	is
	done
as	
the	I
Power	will
behind	be
us.	done.

THE PARTY IS OVER ...

The Twelve Steps of Alcoholics Anonymous

Here are the steps we took, which are
suggested as a program of recovery:

4. Made a searching and fearless moral
inventory of ourselves.

Happy Hour   # Alcoholic

What's your pleasure?   One
the bartender asked.   foot
Indeed, what would it be?   in
Long Island Iced Tea?   the
                                past,

Creme de Menthe frappe?
Or a Black Russian?   one
Perhaps a Tequila Sunrise?   foot
No, safer with a beer.   in
                                the
Definitely not Wild Turkey   future,
on the rocks.
I could end up blacked out   pissing
again in a drunk tank.   on
                                the
Or sitting there on the   present.
toilet
with my feet up.

... AND JUST BEGUN!

The Twelve Steps of Alcoholics Anonymous

Here are the steps we took, which are suggested as a program of recovery:

5. Admitted to God, to ourselves, and to another human being the exact nature of our wrongs.

Normal Is

I don't drink,
normally.

You see,
I did not
get into trouble
every time
I drank,

but every
time I
got into trouble,
I had been
drinking.

I don't drink
normally.

Today

I
will
start
living
from
the
inside
out,

instead
of
from
the
outside
in.

THE PARTY IS OVER ...

The Twelve Steps of Alcoholics Anonymous

Here are the steps we took, which are suggested as a program of recovery:

6. Were entirely ready to have God remove all these defects of character.

Lightning Bolts

Some
of
us
are
illuminated
by
the
light,

most
are
moved
by
the
heat.

Ring around the Ass

You
can
stay
on
the
pity
pot
forever,

as
long
as
you
remember
to
    flush ...

... AND JUST BEGUN!

The Twelve Steps of Alcoholics Anonymous

Here are the steps we took, which are suggested as a program of recovery:

7. Humbly asked Him to remove our shortcomings.

The Fountain

Some
drink
deeply
from
the
fountain
of
knowledge.

Others
just
stand
around
and
gargle.

Suffering

Pain
is
given,

suffering
is
optional.

Get
off
the
cross,

we
need
the
wood.

THE PARTY IS OVER ...

The Twelve Steps of Alcoholics Anonymous

Here are the steps we took, which are suggested as a program of recovery:

8. Made a list of all persons we had harmed, and became willing to make amends to them all.

The Keys

Surrender
to win,
give it away
to keep it,

suffer
to get well,
and die
to live,

ask
to be given,
seek
to find,

and knock
to have opened.

Humility

AA
says
humility
is
not
thinking
less
of
yourself,

but
thinking
of
yourself
less.

... AND JUST BEGUN!

The Twelve Steps of Alcoholics Anonymous

Here are the steps we took, which are suggested as a program of recovery:

9. Made direct amends to such people wherever possible, except when to do so would injure them or others.

Results

If
you
do
what
you've
always
done,

then
you'll
get
what
you
always
got.

Aliens

In
Alcoholics
Anonymous
just
learn
to
relax —

resistance
is
futile,

you
shall
be
assimilated.

THE PARTY IS OVER ...

The Twelve Steps of Alcoholics Anonymous

Here are the steps we took, which are suggested as a program of recovery:

10. Continued to take personal inventory and when we were wrong promptly admitted it.

Little Things

Count to Ten

Confucius
say
it
is
not
the
elephants
that
get
you,

but
those
pesky
ants.

I
continued
to
take
personal
inventory

and
when
I
was
wrong
probably
admitted
it.

... AND JUST BEGUN!

The Twelve Steps of Alcoholics Anonymous

Here are the steps we took, which are suggested as a program of recovery:

11. Sought through prayer and meditation to improve our conscious contact with God as we understood Him, praying only for knowledge of His will for us and the power to carry that out.

Morning

(After sobriety)

Thank you,
my
God,

for
another
good
morning!

(Before sobriety)

Good
God,
it's
morning!

HP's

As
they
say
in
AA—

My
higher
power

can
beat
up

your
higher
power.

THE PARTY IS OVER ...

The Twelve Steps of Alcoholics Anonymous

Here are the steps we took, which are suggested as a program of recovery:

12. Having had a spiritual awakening as the result of these steps, we tried to carry this message to alcoholics, and to practice these principles in all our affairs.

Live

It
is
far
easier

to
preach
the
steps

than
it
is

to
live
them.

Step 12

Remember,
you
are
there

to
carry
the
message

and
not
to
carry

the
alcoholic.

... AND JUST BEGUN!

Many of us exclaimed, "What an order! I can't go through with it." Do not be discouraged. No one among us has been able to maintain anything like perfect adherence to these principles. We are not saints. The point is, that we are willing to grow along spiritual lines.
— *Chapter 5: How It Works, page 60*

Orders

What!
An
order?

I
can't
go

through
with
it.

I
can't
follow

any
orders!

Anonymity

Just
in
case
you
haven't
noticed,

there
is
no
I

in
the
word
anonymous.

THE PARTY IS OVER ...

Our description of the alcoholic, the chapter to the agnostic, and our personal adventures before and after make clear three pertinent ideas:
(a) That we were alcoholic and could not manage our own lives.
(b) That probably no human power could have relieved our alcoholism.
(c) That God could and would if He were sought.
　　— Chapter 5: How It Works, page 60

Help!　　　　　　　Change

Restless, irritable,
and discontent,
or stupid, boring,
and glum.

Cunning, baffling,
and powerful
is vodka, whiskey,
and rum.

For help ask God,
who could and would
if He were sought,

because happy
and joyous and free
can be taught
　　like the ABC's.

If
you
don't
change,

your
sobriety
date
will.

It
works,

if
you
work
it ...

... AND JUST BEGUN!

Selfishness—self-centeredness! That, we think, is the root of our troubles. Driven by a hundred forms of fear, self-delusion, self-seeking, and self-pity, we step on the toes of our fellows and they retaliate.
— *Chapter 5: How It Works, page 62*

Toast

Here's
to
you,

here's
to
me,

if
we
should
ever
disagree,

here's
to
me.

Science

It
is
all
about
mind
over
matter:

I
don't
mind,
and
you
don't
matter.

THE PARTY IS OVER ...

We were now at Step Three. We thought well before taking this step making sure we were ready; that we could at last abandon ourselves utterly to Him. Many of us said to our Maker, as we understood Him ...
 — Chapter 5: How It Works, page 63

Third Step Prayer

God, I offer myself
to Thee—to build with me
and to do with me
as Thou wilt.

Relieve me of the bondage
of self, that I may better
do Thy will.

Take away my difficulties,
that victory over them
may bear witness to those
I would help

of Thy Power, Thy Love,
and Thy Way of life.
May I do Thy will always!

Resentment is the "number one" offender. It destroys more alcoholics than anything else. From it stem all forms of spiritual disease, for we have been not only mentally and physically ill, we have been spiritually sick. When the spiritual malady is overcome, we straighten out mentally and physically.
— *Chapter 5: How It Works, page 64*

Stick with the Winners

You're
rubber
and
I'm
glue,

my
words
bounce
off
you,

and
stick
to ...

who?

Intelligence

I
have
learned
that
artificial
intelligence
is
no
match
at
all

for
natural
stupidity.

THE PARTY IS OVER ...

More than most people, the alcoholic leads a double life. He is very much the actor. To the outer world he presents his stage character. This is the one he likes his fellows to see. He wants to enjoy a certain reputation, but knows in his heart he doesn't deserve it.
— *Chapter6: Into Action, page 73*

Shakespeare said

"All the world's a stage, and all the men and women merely players." He forgot to mention that I was the chief critic. I was always able to see the flaw in every person, every situation.

And I was always glad to point it out, because I knew you wanted perfection, just as I did.

A.A. and acceptance have taught me that there is a bit of good in the worst of us and a bit of bad in the best of us; that we are all children of God.

Mantra

Pet
me,
feed
me,

pet
me,
feed
me,

make
me
feel

like
I
belong.

... AND JUST BEGUN!

We pocket our pride and go to it, illuminating every twist of character, every dark cranny of the past. Once we have taken this step, withholding nothing, we are delighted. We can look the world in the eye. We can be alone at perfect peace and ease.

— Chapter 6: Into Action, page 75

Today

You
can
cherish
the
past

and
dream
about
tomorrow

but
always
live
for
today.

The Years

— for Bruce

Some
of
the
days

can
be
pretty
shitty,

but,
oh,
the
years

are
good!

THE PARTY IS OVER ...

Are we now ready to let God remove from us all the things which we have admitted are objectionable? Can He now take them all—every one? If we still cling to something we will not let go, we ask God to help us be willing. When ready, we say something like this ...
— Chapter 6, Into Action, page 76

Seventh Step Prayer

My Creator,
I am now willing that you
should have all of me,
good and bad.

I pray that you now
remove from me every
single defect of character
which stands in the way
of my usefulness
to you and my fellows.

Grant me strength,
as I go out from here, to do
your bidding.
Amen.

... AND JUST BEGUN!

The alcoholic is like a tornado roaring his way through the lives of others. Hearts are broken. Sweet relationships are dead. Affections have been uprooted. Selfish and inconsiderate habits have kept the home in turmoil. We feel a man is unthinking when he says that sobriety is enough. He is like the farmer who came up out of his cyclone cellar to find his home ruined. To his wife, he remarked, "Don't see anything the matter here, Ma. Ain't it grand the wind stopped blowin'?"
 — *Chapter 6: Into Action, page 82*

Theory	Tornado
Into	Don't
Action:	see
The	anything
spiritual	the
life	matter
is	here,
not	Ma.
a	
theory.	Ain't
	it
We	grand
have	the
to	wind
live	stopped
it.	blowin'?

THE PARTY IS OVER ...

If we are painstaking about this phase of our development, we will be amazed before we are half way through ... Are these extravagant promises? We think not. They are being fulfilled among us — sometimes quickly, sometimes slowly. They will always materialize if we work for them.
  — Chapter 6: Into Action, pages 83-84

The Promises

We are going to know a new freedom and a new happiness.

We will not regret the past nor wish to shut the door on it.

We will comprehend the word serenity and we will know peace.

No matter how far down the scale we have gone, we will see how our experience can benefit others.

That feeling of uselessness and self-pity will disappear.

We will lose interest in selfish things and gain interest in our fellows.

Self-seeking will slip away.

... AND JUST BEGUN!

Our whole attitude and outlook upon life will change.

Fear of people and of economic insecurity will leave us.

We will intuitively know how to handle situations which used to baffle us.

We will suddenly realize that God is doing for us what we could not do for ourselves.

THE PARTY IS OVER ...

Practical experience shows that nothing will so much insure immunity from drinking as intensive work with other alcoholics. It works when other activities fail. This is our twelfth suggestion: Carry this message to other alcoholics! You can help when no one else can.
   --- *Chapter 7: Working with Others, page 89*

Like you,
Like me

Like Freud
I spend a lot of time
   thinking of sex,

Like Moses
I spend a lot of time
   in denial,

like Lipton,
I spend a lot of time
   in my cups,

like Jesus,
I spend a lot of time
   on the cross,

like Jim Beam,
I spend a lot of time
   in the bottle,

like Brunswick,
I spend a lot of time
   in the gutter,

like Bill Wilson
I spend a lot of time
   in meetings.

... AND JUST BEGUN!

We have traveled a rocky road, there is no mistake about that. We have had long rendezvous with hurt pride, frustration, self-pity, misunderstanding and fear. These are not pleasant companions. We have been driven to maudlin sympathy, to bitter resentment. Some of us veered from extreme to extreme, ever hoping that one day our loved ones would be them- selves once more.
— *"To Wives" pages 104-05*

A Prayer

Dear Lord,

I pray
for Wisdom
to understand
my man;

Love
to forgive him;
And Patience
for his moods;

Because Lord,
if I pray
for strength,
I will beat him
 to death.

Amen

Cleopatra

The
queen
of
denial

drank
a
lot

and
made
an
asp

out
of
herself.

THE PARTY IS OVER ...

Patience, tolerance, understanding and love are the watchwords. Show him these things in yourself and they will be reflected back to you from him. Live and let live is the rule. If you both show a willingness to remedy your own defects, there will be little need to criticize each other.
— Chapter 8: To Wives, page 118

More Baloney

The recovering alcoholic
opened his lunch box,
looked inside, and said,
Another baloney sandwich!

This went on all week long,
until finally on Friday,
he chucked the sandwich
against the wall.

His buddy asked him,
Why don't you tell your wife
that you're tired of eating
baloney every day?

What wife? I'm not married.
I make my own lunches.

Alanon

Maybe
the
grace
of
God
entered
your
wife

and
then
it
entered
your
life.

... AND JUST BEGUN!

Our women folk have suggested certain attitudes a wife may take with the husband who is recovering. Perhaps they created the impression that he is to be wrapped in cotton wool and placed on a pedestal. Successful readjustment means the opposite.
— *Chapter 9: The Family Afterward, page 122*

Today

You
cannot
change
the
past,

but
you can
make
today

a
better
yesterday

for
tomorrow.

AA Prayer

God,
please
keep
one
hand
on
my
shoulder

and
the
other
over
my
mouth.

THE PARTY IS OVER …

Cessation of drinking is but the first step away from a highly strained, abnormal condition. A doctor said to us, "Years of living with an alcoholic is almost sure to make any wife or child neurotic. The entire family is, to some extent, ill." Let families realize, as they start their journey, that all will not be fair weather.
— Chapter 9: The Family Afterward, page 122

Families

My
family
tree
should
have
been
cut
down

and
turned
into
a
stop
  sign.

Parents

Relax
because
your
children
will
still
get
arrested

and
be
in
the
local
    paper.

> *But we aren't a glum lot. If newcomers could see no joy or fun in our existence, they wouldn't want it. We absolutely insist on enjoying life. We try not to indulge in cynicism over the state of the nations, nor do we carry the world's troubles on our shoulders.*
> *Chapter 9: The Family Afterward, page 132*

The result

was
Neil
until
we
let
go
absolutely,

now
we
smile
at
such
a
Sally.

Bob Forde

You
spell
my
name
Forde
with
an
E,

and
Bob
with
just
one
O.

THE PARTY IS OVER ...

When dealing with an alcoholic, there may be a natural annoyance that a man could be so weak, stupid and irresponsible. Even when you understand the malady better, you may feel this feeling rising. A look at the alcoholic in your organization is many times illuminating. Is he not usually brilliant, fast- thinking, imaginative and likeable? When sober, does he not work hard and have a knack of getting things done?
— Chapter 10: To Employers, pages 139-40

Purpose

The
good
Lord
didn't
create
anything
without
a
purpose,

but
drunks
come
pretty
close.

The Hustler

Alcohol let me win
every now and then
just to keep
me coming back.

We played for fun,
a beer at first,
then whiskey said,
    Go ahead!

I lost my money,
I lost my car,
I lost my house,
I lost my wife,

and the, when I tried
to quit, I almost
    lost my life.

... AND JUST BEGUN!

For most normal folks, drinking means conviviality, companionship and colorful imagination. It means release from care, boredom and worry. It is joyous intimacy with friends and a feeling that life is good. But not so with us in those last days of heavy drinking. The old pleasures were gone. They were but memories.
— Chapter 11: Vision for You, page 151

Vision for You

You
Take
the
Path

of
Least
Resistance,

I'll
Trudge
the
Road

of
Happy
Destiny.

Horsemen

The
hideous
Four
Horsemen —

Terror,
Bewilderment,
Frustration,
Despair.

He
will
wish
for
the
end.

THE PARTY IS OVER ...

Yes, there is a substitute and it is vastly more than that. It is a fellowship in Alcoholics Anonymous. There you will find release from care, boredom and worry. Your imagination will be ?red. Life will mean something at last. The most satisfactory years of your existence lie ahead. Thus we find the fellowship, and so will you.
— Chapter 11: Vision for You, page 152

The Road of Happy Destiny

Nudge means to poke
   something into action,
budge means to move
   something an inch or two,
judge means to decide
   something should move,
grudge means to be mad
   something moved you,

fudge means to lie about,
   lying about moving,
drudge is a person
   who will not budge,
but, finally, and you knew
   it was coming —
trudge means to move
   forward with purpose.

... AND JUST BEGUN!

The Stories

All changes made over the years in the Big Book (A.A. members' fond nickname for this volume) have had the same purpose: to represent the current membership of Alcoholics Anonymous more accurately, and thereby to reach more alcoholics. If you have a drinking problem, we hope that you may pause in reading one of the forty-two personal stories and think: "Yes, that happened to me"; or, more important, "Yes, I've felt like that"; or, most important, "Yes, I believe this program can work for me too."
— Preface to the Fourth Edition

The Way Out

I learned how to smoke
when it seemed sophisticated,
and I learned how to drink
when the wine was carbonated,

I learned how to dance
when the couple never spoke,
I learned about escape
when I took that first toke,

I learned how to party
in a group, but stay all alone,
I learned how to live
while intoxicated and stoned,

THE PARTY IS OVER ...

I learned how to say
that I was having great fun
when, in reality,
I was having none.

I learned how to tell the truth
when I could no longer lie,
I learned how to quit
when I thought I would die,

I learned how to get sober,
to smile and to fake it,
until I learned to live sober
and really make it,

I learned how to stop saying
that I was doing fine,
when I learned how to pray
for God's will, not mine.

... AND JUST BEGUN!

I was born in a small New England village of about seven thousand souls. The general moral standard was, as I recall it, far above the average. No beer or liquor was sold in the neighborhood, except at the State liquor agency where perhaps one might procure a pint if he could convince the agent that he really needed it. Without this proof the expectant purchaser would be forced to depart empty handed with none of what I later came to believe was the great panacea for all human ills
— "Doctor Bob's Nightmare" page 171

I Believe

I could not hear
what I could not hear,

I could not see
what I could not see,

I could not know
what I could not know,

I could not feel
what I could not feel,

until my ears
and eyes were open,

until my mind and
heart were open,

only then could I
come to believe.

THE PARTY IS OVER ...

Despite great opportunities, alcohol nearly ended her life. An early member, she spread the word among women in our pioneering period.
 — *"Women Suffer, Too" page 200*

"Blanks"

What was I saying ...
from far away, as if in a delirium,
I heard my own voice—calling
someone "Dorothy," talking
of dress shops, of jobs ...

the words came clearer ...
this sound of my own voice frightened
me as it came closer ...
and suddenly, there I was, talking of
I knew not what,
to someone I'd never seen before
that very moment.

Abruptly I stopped speaking.
Where was I?

... AND JUST BEGUN!

That was the point at which my doctor gave me the book Alcoholics Anonymous to read. The first chapters were a revelation to me. I wasn't the only person in the world who felt and behaved like this! ... I was suffering from an actual disease that had a name and symptoms like diabetes or cancer or TB—and a disease was respectable, not a moral stigma! But ... I couldn't stomach religion, and I didn't like the mention of God or any of the other capital letters. If that was the way out, it wasn't for me.
— *"Women Suffer, Too" page 205*

Thy Will Be Done

I get my greatest thrill
of accomplishment from the knowledge
that I have played a part
in the new happiness achieved by
countless others like myself.
The fact that I can work again
and earn my living is important but
secondary.

I believe that my once overweening
self-will has finally found
its proper place, for I can say
many times daily, "Thy will be done,
not mine"...
and mean it.

THE PARTY IS OVER ...

A little more than fifteen years ago, through a long and calamitous series of shattering experiences, I found myself being helplessly propelled toward total destruction. I was without power to change the course my life had taken. How I had arrived at this tragic impasse, I could not have explained to anyone. I was thirty-three years old and my life was spent. I was caught in a cycle of alcohol and sedation that was proving inescapable, and consciousness had become intolerable.
— *"The Keys of the Kingdom" page 268*

Keys of the Kingdom

There is no more aloneness,
with that awful ache,
so deep in the heart
of every alcoholic

that nothing, before, could
ever reach it. That ache
is gone and never need
return again.

Now there is a sense
of belonging, of being wanted
and needed and loved.

In return for a bottle
and a hangover, we have been
given the Keys of the Kingdom.

... AND JUST BEGUN!

They suggested I could just stay sober one day at a time. They explained that it might be easier to set my sights on the twenty- four hours in front of me and to take on these other situations when and if they ever arrived. I decided to give sobriety a try, one day at a time, and I've done it that way ever since.
— "The Missing Link" 286-87

Today

You
can
cherish
the
past

and
dream
about
tomorrow

but
always
live
for
today.

Alcoholic

One
foot
in
the
past,

one
foot
in
the
future,

pissing
on
the
present.

Denial is the most cunning, baffling, and powerful part of my disease, the disease of alcoholism. When I look back now, it's hard to imagine I didn't see a problem with my drinking. But instead of seeing the truth when all of the "yets" (as in, that hasn't happened to me—yet) started happening, I just kept lowering my standards.
— *"Crossing the River of Denial" page 328*

Scene of the Crime

Bottle of booze
on Halloween night,
intuitive thought
of a Budweiser lite.

I drew up the plans,
and plotted a crime
in an old gin mill,
drinking Gallo wine.

I told my buddies
we'd face no harm,
but being drunk
I'd forgot the alarm.

We tried to run
but Sheriff got us,
so we just lied like
mama taught us,

the judge asked what
were you thinking?
We told him we'd
just been drinking.

He gave us two years
in the county jail
and said to forget
any thoughts of bail.

So here I sit
in this tiny cell,
just one notch better
than going to hell.

The warden told me
about AA they had,
but I said, Shoot,
I ain't that bad!

... AND JUST BEGUN!

This poem is dedicated to Cleve L., a member of the Sequim, Washington, Early Birds, who died in 2014 with 53 years of continuous sobriety.

Beatitudes for Boozers

— for Cleve

Blessed is the man who has nothing to say
    and cannot be persuaded to say it.

Blessed is the alcoholic who overcomes
    the desire to whine.

Blessed are the meek, for they shall be
    the new group secretaries.

Blessed are they who stay, for they shall
    learn to pray.

Blessed are they who open the meetings
    early, for they shall inherit the
    newcomers.

Blessed are the newcomers, for they shall
    find what was lost.

Blessed are the poor in spirits, for they
    shall inherit the kingdom of God.

Blessed are the Scotts, for theirs shall be
    a great gathering of the clan.

THE PARTY IS OVER ...

Blessed are the Irish, for where two or
   three are gathered, you will surely
   find a fifth.

Blessed are the Germans and the Dutch,
   for they will learn that beer really
   is a form of alcohol.

Blessed are they who have done hard
   time, for they shall be set free.

Blessed are they who get into service,
   for theirs is all the glory.

Blessed are the sponsors, for they shall
   be given the words of the people.

Blessed are they who reach out the hand
   of friendship, for their lives will
   never be empty.

Blessed is the GSR who can attend service
   meetings without getting into
   a fist fight.

Blessed is the group treasurer who can
   serve a full term without having
   to flee the state.

Blessed are they who hunger and thirst
   after sobriety, for they will surely be filled
   with coffee and donuts.

... AND JUST BEGUN!

Blessed are the pure in heart, for they
  shall find a reserved seat right up front in
  open meetings.

Blessed are they who have reached the
  end of the rope, for they will fall
  into a great fellowship.

Blessed are the restless, irritable,
  and discontent, for they will surely
  know peace.

THE PARTY IS OVER ...

My writing career was described in the couplet "Alcohol gave me wings to fly, / And then it took away the sky."

... What alcoholic can live with rejection? How devastating, too, are the subsequent feelings of inadequacy and self-pity. There's only one answer — liquid comfort.

— "Those Golden Years" 3rd edition, page 331

Those Golden Years

Liquor
gave
me
the
wings
to
fly,

and
then
it
took
away
the
sky.

Circe says

The
difference
between
pigs
and
men

is
pigs
don't
turn
into
men

when
they
    drink.

... AND JUST BEGUN!

If there ever was anyone who came to A.A. by mistake, it was I. I just didn't belong here. Never in my wildest moments had it occurred to me that I might like to be an alcoholic.
— *"Doctor, Alcoholic, Addict" 3rd Edition, pages 439 and 449*

Acceptance

is the answer to all my problems today. When I am disturbed, it is because I find some person, place, thing, or situation —

some fact of my life — unacceptable to me, and I can find no serenity until I accept that person, place, thing, or situation

as being exactly the way it is supposed to be at this moment. Nothing, absolutely nothing, happens in God's world by mistake.

Until I could accept my alcoholism, I could not stay sober; unless I accept life completely on life's terms, I cannot be happy.

I need to concentrate not so much on what needs to be changed in the world as on what needs to be changed in me and
    in my attitudes.

THE PARTY IS OVER ...

I proud to be son of Tall Man, American Indian, and member of A.A. for many moons. We all one as Great Spirit walks through A.A. like sun walks through day. This first story I ever write. Sorry for mistakes. Love has no words to spell or lines to start and stop. Our language has few words to say many things.
— *"Join the Tribe" 3rd edition, page 474*

Join the Tribe

Don't
be afraid
to join A.A.

I once
hear
people say

only
Indians
crazy
when drunk.

If so,
A.A. full
of Indians.
Join the tribe!

Humble

With tireless
devotion
and humility,
this venerable
Indian gentleman
traveled
thousands
of miles humbly
pleading
    for sobriety.

He planted many
seeds and it will be
many moons
before another rises
to walk
    in his shoes.

... AND JUST BEGUN!

God willing, we members of A.A. may never again have to deal with drinking, but we have to deal with sobriety every day. How do we do it? By learning— through practicing the Twelve Steps and through shar- ing at meetings—how to cope with the problems that we looked to booze to solve, back in our drinking days.
— *"To Handle Sobriety" page 559*

Reality

I lived
in a dream world.
A.A. led me
gently from this
fantasizing
to embrace
reality
with open arms.

And I found
it beautiful!
For at last, I was
at peace
with myself.
And with others.
And with God.

Fantasy

Reality
is
merely
an
illusion
that
is
caused

by
the
lack
of
sufficient
alcohol.

THE PARTY IS OVER ...

To those now in its fold, Alcoholics Anonymous has made the difference between misery and sobriety, and often the difference between life and death. A.A. can, of course, mean just as much to uncounted alcoholics not yet reached.
— *Appendix I: The A.A. Tradition, page 560*

First and Last

Tradition One — Our common welfare should come first;

personal recovery depends upon A.A. unity.

Anonymity is

the spiritual foundation of all our Traditions,

ever reminding us to place principles before personalities.

... AND JUST BEGUN!

Therefore, no society of men and women ever had a more urgent need for continuous effectiveness and permanent unity. We alcoholics see that we must work together and hang together, else most of us will finally die alone.
— *Appendix I: The A.A. Tradition, page 560*

Honesty

If
all
of
us

do
not
hang
together,

we
will
surely
all

hang
separately.

AA Wisdom

A man walks
down the street
and falls
into a hole.

The next day
he sees the hole
but still
falls into it.

The third day
he walks around
the hole.

On the fourth
day
he takes
another street.

THE PARTY IS OVER ...

The terms "spiritual experience" and "spiritual awakening" are used many times in this book which, upon careful reading, shows that the personality change sufficient to bring about recovery from alcoholism has manifested itself among us in many different forms.
  — Appendix II: Spiritual Experience

Look Within

With few exceptions our
members find that they
have tapped an unsuspected
inner resource which
they presently identify
with their own conception
of a Power greater
than themselves.

Most of us think this
awareness of a Power greater
than ourselves is the essence
of spiritual experience.
Our more religious members
call it "God-consciousness."

Sermon

I'd
rather
see
a
sermon
than
hear
one,

what
you
do

speaks
louder
than

words.

... AND JUST BEGUN!

We find that no one need have difficulty with the spirituality of the program. Willingness, honesty and open mindedness are the essentials of recovery. But these are indispensable.
— *Appendix II: Spiritual Experience*

Herbert Spencer

There is
a principle
which is a bar
against all
information,

which is proof
against all
arguments
and which cannot
fail to keep a man

in everlasting
ignorance — that
principle
is contempt prior
to investigation.

William Arthur Ward

The
pessimist
complains
about
the wind;

the
optimist
expects
it
to change;

the
realist
adjusts
the sails.

THE PARTY IS OVER ...

Bar Life

Indeed, I am
the center
of the universe.

How could
it be any other
way?

Like rings
on a dart board,
I send ripples

around the room,
and the world
sends back

darts as my sole
reward.

... AND JUST BEGUN!

"The Way Out" was originally to be the title of the Big Book of Alcoholics Anonymous, but it had already been used, several times. Following is a "found poem" where lines are taken from each of the 11 chapters:

The Way Out

Once we landed in England,
we were rocketed
 into a 4th dimension.

Take a trip, not take a trip,
lack of power,
 that was our dilemma.

For who has thoroughly
followed our path?
 Pocket our pride, go to it.

But sometimes it is wise
to wait, for we have traveled
 a rocky road.

Better wrapped in cotton,
or to be placed on a pedestal?
 Leave it alone!

Join us, and trudge the road
 of happy destiny.

THE PARTY IS OVER ...

Afterword

I hope you've enjoyed this book. The whole purpose is to "promote" the Happy, Joyous and Free attitude of Alcoholics Anonymous. Of course, "attraction" is the guide-word, so, if you liked any of the poems, try to copy down some that you hear in your own meetings. You will be amazed at how many AA one-liners can be put into the form of 14 words or 14 lines. Shakespeare would be proud!

Jim F

Jim

A
shot
of
whiskey
in
a
glass
of
milk?

We
call
this
plain
insanity!

See what I mean? I think each of us can find ourselves in the Big Book, if we look hard enough ...

The Party Is Over ... and Just Begun!

Made in the USA
Las Vegas, NV
14 January 2023